AIDEN MASH

DIGITAL GOLD

**The Beginner's Guide to Digital Product Success,
Learn Useful Tips and Methods on How to Create
Digital Products and Earn Massive Profits**

Descrierea CIP a Bibliotecii Naționale a României
AIDEN MASH
    DIGITAL GOLD. The Beginner's Guide to Digital Product Success, Learn Useful Tips and Methods on How to Create Digital Products and Earn Massive Profits / Aiden Mash – Bucharest: Editura My Ebook, 2021
    ISBN

AIDEN MASH

DIGITAL GOLD

The Beginner's Guide to Digital Product Success, Learn Useful Tips and Methods on How to Create Digital Products and Earn Massive Profits

My Ebook Publishing House
Bucharest, 2021

TABLE OF CONTENTS

INTRODUCTION

When it comes to making money online and profiting from your website, one of the most reliable strategies is to sell products. Yes, you can make money with ads or affiliate programs, but if steady streams of income that you can count on are your goal, having your own paid products is the way to go.

That being said, it can be expensive and a bit risky to offer your own products for sale. This applies in particular when you're talking about physical products. You have to buy the inventory, store it, and then ship it out to customers. Not only does it take a substantial investment on your part (and a risk if the products don't end up selling), it's also quite a bit of extra work to ship and handle each item.

Digital products, on the other hand, are easy to create, easy to store, and you can sell the same item over and over again. It's a lot more scalable and an excellent way to generate a reliable income from your online presence. It's also what this guide is all about. Over the coming pages and chapters, I'll show you what digital products are and why you should create them, how to create info products that your audience wants and needs, how to create your first digital product, and how to expand on this idea so you can keep working away on creating your very own digital product empire.

Along the way, there will be plenty of tips and ideas to get started, make things easier, and most importantly make this entire effort more profitable. I recommend you read this guide with a notebook in hand to take notes and jot down ideas as they come up.

By far the most important job for you is to take action. This short guide won't do you any good if you sit on the information and don't do anything with it. I would like to challenge you to start working on your first digital product as soon as you're done reading the guide. In fact, read it with the intent to have your first product launched within a month (or even earlier). Start thinking about the products you can create as you read it and then get to work. The only thing standing between you and your first digital product that makes you money is action.

Ready to get started? Let's start by taking a look at what these digital or information products I've been talking about are and what you can create yourself.

What Are Digital Products

Let's dive a little deeper and talk about what exactly digital products are, what different types you may want to consider putting together for your audience, and the likes. As you read through this chapter, you may start to come up with potential product ideas. Jot them down, so you have something to brainstorm and work from throughout the coming chapters.

The main reason digital products are such a great way to make offers to your target audience, your website visitors, blog readers, and email subscribers is that they are products you can create yourself. There's no overhead. There's no long product development and testing process.

There's no warehouses and shipping department to worry about. They are products that your customers purchase online and then download.

I'm sure you've come across plenty of free and paid digital products already. They are the short reports or audio/video recordings you get as a "Thank You" for signing up for someone's email list. It's the eBook you bought on a website ages ago to learn how to get your baby to sleep through the night. It's the video tutorial course you signed up for to figure out how to use Facebook ads. And of course, the report you're reading right now is a digital product.

In essence, digital products are bought and downloaded online. Most of them are information products. The big advantage is that they are created once and can then be sold again and again. This means that a digital product business is very scalable. Once you have your product, it's not much harder to sell 1,000 copies than it is to sell 5. That's what makes it so attractive to online marketers and solo entrepreneurs. It's not terribly complicated to get into the information product business, yet you can scale it up to make big money by creating more products and reaching larger and larger audiences.

With information products, you end up spending a fairly short amount of time in the beginning to create your product, and then shift focus and spend almost all your time marketing it going forward. Until you're ready to create the next product. This is a very good thing because it allows you to focus on and learn how to do this one step at a time. It's yet another reason why it is such a good type of product to produce.

Let's wrap this first chapter up with a quick look at the different types of digital products out there. What they all have in common is that they are a way to share content and information with the people who are looking for it or need it to reach their goals.

EBooks and Short Reports

One of the easiest digital products for most people to create is an eBook or short report. The eBook you're reading right now is the perfect example of this. The content is usually written in a text editor or word processor like Google Docs, or Microsoft Word. It is then turned into a pdf and uploaded to the web. Customers can then download the pdf after they purchase the product.

The big advantages of this type of product are that it's easy to create with software most of us have and are comfortable to use. It's also easy to change and update the product down the road. You simply go back to your original Word document, changing it as needed, creating a new pdf, and uploading it to replace the old version. If your preferred method of content creation is writing, this is the way to go.

Audio Books and Audio Courses

If you're not comfortable typing out your product, or you know that your target audience prefers to listen to content over reading it, audio products can be a great choice. They also make a high-value addition to your written eBook. Record yourself reading your eBook for an audio book component to your digital product that adds a lot of perceived value.

Another option is to create an audio course where you walk students through each lesson in audio recordings. You can create checklists and handouts to go along with the audio content.

Video Courses And Webinars

A third option is creating video products. You can create a video course and record each lesson either via screen capture software or by recording yourself talk using your webcam, phone, or even your digital camera. You edit and upload these videos to your site and deliver them to your customers who can either download or stream the videos. If you go this route, I recommend you create short individual lessons over one long video. It makes it easier to upload, download, and consume. It also makes it much easier for you to go back and change one little video instead of the whole thing when you need to make changes.

Of course, live webinars and webinar recordings make another attractive video product. You invite your customers to join you live and then also provide them with the recording later. It's a fun format that allows you to create your digital content on the fly and interact with your target audience.

Checklists And Printables

Last but not least let's talk about a quick and easy product you can create out of checklists and printables. People like things that make their lives easier from printable meal plans and shopping lists to checklists for setting up their first blog. Tap into this need by compiling the information and presenting it in an easy to use format. Checklists and printables also make great addition or bonuses to any other digital products.

Of course, this isn't a complete list of what you can do with digital information products. You could also create apps or software, develop custom spreadsheets and the likes. It's simply a list of some of the most common and easy to create digital products. It's a starting point for you, and of course, you can mix and match these products to fit your needs and those of your target audience. Which brings us to chapter two which is where we'll explore what your potential customers want and need.

What Does Your Audience Want And Need

Now that you know a little more about the different types of digital products you can create, you may be tempted to jump in, pick a format, and get to work. There's one more piece of information you need first, which is what your audience wants and needs. It's important to realize that the two aren't always the same. What your audience wants and what they need to know or work on next can be related, but can also be very different. For example, your potential customers may want an easy way to add an extra $1,000 to their bottom line, but that they need a way to build a list so they can get more repeat business. In that case, your goal is to sell them a product that teaches them how to make an extra grand with a mailing list. But let's not get ahead of ourselves. Before you can get into your audience's wants and needs, you need to know who your target audience and ideal customers are.

Define Your Target Audience

Your first job is to figure out who your target audience is. Once you know that, you'll have a much better idea of what your product should be about and even what format will work best for the majority of your potential customers.

Start with the niche you're in and then sub-niche it and get as specific as possible. For example, you may decide to create content and information products for local small businesses. You can get even more specific and decide that you want to work with people who have a web presence but are looking for ways to increase their business and their bottom line through online channels. They are the local restaurants, realtors, hair salons, flower shops, etc. who want to learn how to grow a list, get email subscribers into the store, grow their reach on social media, and make it easy to be found online through a Google search. That's the kind of specific picture of your target audience that you want to create. In this scenario, you may also want to define them as people who are interested in learning how to do these things themselves instead of hiring a social media and email manager. There's a big difference between the two and one group will be interested in your info products, while the other is looking or a "done for you" service.

Solve A Problem Or Entertain

There are two big motivators that get us to purchase a digital product. One is entertainment, and the other is problem-solving. Think about the digital products you've bought in the past. Your Netflix subscription and most of the books on your Kindle are there to entertain you. This guide on digital product creation, on the other hand, helps you solve to problem of making money online (or at least part of the problem). As you start to think about other digital products you've bought, you'll quickly see that they all neatly into one of these two categories. Every once in a while a product may hit on both, but that's rare and not always possible to do.

For our purposes, we want to create a digital product that's either highly entertaining (like a novel for example) or one that helps our customers solve a problem. For most of us, the focus will be on problem-solving products. Here are a few examples to give you an idea of the type of product we're talking about:

- Get your baby to sleep through the night.
- How to cook a healthy dinner in 30 minutes or less.
- Pay off your student loan in record time.

- Write compelling blog posts that grab your reader's attention.

- Start your online business on a tight budget.

- Grow your reach through social media.

- Negotiate a bigger paycheck.

Your primary job as an info product creator is to define or find a problem your target audience has and then provide them with the information and tools they need to solve said problem.

Don't Be Afraid To Be Specific

Last but not least, don't be afraid to be very specific with your digital products. Let's go back to the earlier example of providing digital products to local business owners who want to increase the business they get as a result of their online marketing efforts. It could be a very smart choice to target individual types of businesses. For example, you could create a product about starting and profiting from a mailing list for flower shops. Or how about Facebook advertising strategies for flower shops. You can get very specific in the strategies and examples you use throughout your product. As a result, it will be much easier to sell this particular product to brick and mortar flower shops.

Since everything is digital, there's no reason you can't go back and edit the product later on, so it's a good fit for local restaurant owners or hair salons. The bulk of the content will be the same, and you just tweak it to fit this new audience. But let's not get ahead of ourselves. Before you can think about repurposing and retargeting your products, it's time to get that first one under your belt. That's exactly what the next chapter is all about.

What I want you to take away from this chapter is that you need to know who your target audience and your ideal customers are, what problems they have, and how you can help them solve one of those problems. Once you figure this out, the actual product creating will become pretty straight-forward.

Creating Your First Digital Product

I'm sure you're ready to dive in and finally get to work on your first digital product. Before we dive into the actual how-to, I have one piece of valuable advice for you. Start with something fairly small and quick to put together. You want to get the basics down and have that introductory product up for sale as fast as possible. Don't bog yourself down with the details of a large product or course. That can come later.

If it helps, think of this as your practice product. You're getting comfortable with the process and all the little steps it takes to take a digital product from idea to finished product up for purchase on your site. Some people have a hard time with this first product and feel that it has to be perfect and all-encompassing. It doesn't. Remember, this is digital which make it easy to change spelling errors, correct information, clear up a section, and of course, add to it later on.

The most important thing right now is to get that first product under your belt. Pick something easy to talk or write about and keep the product fairly small. If you're still feeling stuck or can't get yourself to start because you feel that it has to be perfect, tell yourself you're only creating this for practice and that it will never see the light of day. Who knows, after it's done, you may decide to put it up for sale or a few dollars to see how it does. Take the pressure off for now and get into product creation mode.

Decide On Your Topic

If you've been taking notes and jotting down ideas as you were working through this report, you probably already have a short list of product ideas and topics. If not, spend a few minutes right now reviewing the chapter on what your audience wants and needs and come up with a few ideas.

Narrow it down and decide on a particular topic for your first info product. Again, don't make it too broad. Instead of teaching your audience all there is to know about baby care, pick something like how to introduce your baby to solid foods, or how to get your baby to sleep through the night. Instead of creating a massive course with everything there is to know about getting traffic to your website, create a small product with one specific strategy like using Linked In to send targeted traffic to your blog for example.

Pick A Format

Once you have your topic, it's time to decide on a format. Do you want to write an eBook like the one you're reading right now, record an audiobook, host a webinar, or film a video tutorial?

The key is to make it easy on yourself the first go around. If you're comfortable creating a document in MS Word or Google Docs and then converting it into a pdf chose that. If you're better with your video camera or a microphone, go the video or audio route. Choose something that's easy to create so you don't get frustrated with too much technical stuff. If you find that your audience doesn't respond well to the format you chose (something you won't know for sure until you put it up for sale), you can always go back and convert it to a different or additional format down the road. You can write your eBook as text and then do an audio version down the road.

Create The Content

Next, comes the most time-consuming portion of this exercise. It's time to create the actual product, and that means content creation. I find it helpful to start with an outline of what I want to cover. The table of contents for this book is pretty much what my outline for this eBook looked like.

With that in place, it's simply a matter of filling in the blanks and sharing the information with your readers. Set aside a little time each day to work on this. It's also very helpful to set yourself a deadline. If you give yourself a month to write a short 6,000 word eBook like this, it will take you at least that long. If you give yourself a weekend, you'll look yourself in your office, make a bunch of coffee and get it done.

Once it's all written, walk away from it for a bit and then come back and edit. Fix any mistakes and spelling errors you can find. Then read everything again (or listen, or watch), and make sure it flows well and makes sense to you. Don't be too nitpicky, but make sure it's a quality product that will be of use to others. If you chose a video or audio format, you'll be doing editing to get the final version of your recording.

If you're unsure about the quality of your product when it's all done, or you're nervous about putting it out there (we all are with the first few products), hand it to a good friend, colleague, or virtual assistant for review. In fact, it may not be a bad idea to hand out a few review copies not only for feedback but also to gather testimonials for your sales page – which we'll cover in more detail a little further on in the process.

Create Downloadable Files

Once you have your product created and edited, it's time to get in into a downloadable format that you can upload to your website and that your customers will be able to download and consume down the road.

For word documents like eBooks, short reports, checklists, and printables this will usually be a PDF document. Your word processing program should be able to let you convert to pdf.

Audio files can be delivered as mp3 files, or you can allow customers to stream the audio from your site. For video, you also have several options. You can have them download the mp4 (or whatever your preferred video format is) file, or you can create a private, unlisted, or even password protected video on a site like YouTube or Vimeo. A third option is to host the video on a site like this and then embed the video on your download page. This works particularly well if you have other files that customers can download to go along with the video like a handout or checklist for example.

Decide how you want to format the finished product. If it's a large product or something that includes several files, it may be a good idea to zip them and allow customers to download everything in one zip file. Last but not least, provide them with some basic information of what software they will need to open and view the files to cut down on customer service emails after the sale.

Let's Talk About Infrastructure

Once you have your product finished and packaged up, it's time to get some infrastructure in place so people can buy your product. You need a page to tell them what it's about (the sales page), a buy button, and some way to collect payments, and of course a download page where they can grab the file or files you created in the last section. Let's look at each of these components one by one.

The Sales Page

The page where you share what you have to offer is the sales page. This can be as long and complicated as you want it to be. For your first product, which should be a lower priced product, I suggest you keep it simple and keep it short.

Start with an attention-grabbing headline. This should pull the reader in and focus on what they want or the problem they need to solve. Follow that with a little introduction where you transition from what they want to what they need. Add a few bullet points to let them know exactly what they are getting. You could share pieces of your product outline, or highlight a few benefits from the product. Always focus on what's in it for your customers and highlight benefits instead of features.

Wrap it up with a call to action where you specifically ask your reader to buy and then, of course, a buy button. If you want you can put one more reminder, a guarantee or a notice about the fact that the product will be delivered as soon as they buy. That's it. Keep it simple, to start. As with your product, you can always go back and tweak the sales page later with feedback from your customers and to test to see what's working best.

The Download Page

The next piece of the puzzle is the download page. This is usually a pretty simple and straightforward page to create. Start by thanking your customers for their purchase.

Next, you want to give them access to the products they just bought. This is usually a link to the finished file, be it pdf, mp3, mp4, or zip file. If you're streaming audio or video content, embed it on this page.

It's also helpful to let them know how to download the content (right- click to save the pdf for example) and point them to software to open the file with like Adobe reader for PDFs and a media player for audio and video. The easier you make it for them, the fewer question you'll have to answer later.

Speaking of which, start collecting these questions once your offer is up and running and add both the most common questions and your answers to a FAQ (Frequently Asked Questions) page and link to it along with your contact page from the download page

A Way To Pay

Your sales page will include a buy button, and you obviously need a way to take payments for your digital products online. There are quite a few different ways to do this. We take a look at three different options here. I recommend you start with a simple PayPal button, to begin with, and then change it up as and when you need more functionality. Start making some money so you can invest it into some of the other options.

Start With PayPal

The easiest way to create a start button is with PayPal. You probably already have an account. It's a very straightforward process, and PayPal has some great step by step instructions here:

https://developer.paypal.com/docs/classic/paypal-payments-standard/ integration-guide/buy_now_step_1/

Follow those to create your button. At the end of the process, you'll have some code that you can copy and paste into the appropriate spots on your sales page. If your sales page is short, one button should do. If it is relatively long, consider adding multiple buy buttons, so customers don't have to scroll all the way to the bottom of the page to purchase.

Hosted Payment Options Like Clickbank or JVZoo

If you want a little more functionality and most importantly if you want an affiliate program for your product so other people can help you promote and get a commission for each sale, sites like Clickbank and JVZoo are your best bet.

They take care of the sales process, affiliate tracking, paying affiliates for you for a small fee and a portion of the profits. It's an inexpensive way to get started, and for most people, this has everything they need going forward. Plenty six figure info product sellers grow their business exclusively through these platforms.

Your Own Shopping Cart Software

The biggest advantage of having your own shopping cart software is that you have more control over your customer lists. You can also do more with this type of software as far as targeted mailings, subscription payments, special offers, and combo discounts are concerned. Most good shopping cart software will also give you the ability to set up an affiliate program so others can help you market and promote.

Popular options for shopping cart software include 1 Shopping Cart, Shopify, Woo Cart, Amember, and Infusionsoft. Do your homework and pick an option that you think works for what you want to do and is within your budget.

Make Your Offer Live And Start Sending Traffic To It

Once you have your sales page, download page, and a way for customers to pay set up, it's time to make your offer live. Push the Publish button on your pages if you haven't already done so and then test your offer.

This is an important part of every product launch that's often forgotten. No matter how careful you are or how good you think you've gotten at this, you will make mistakes. This initial test purchase is the time to catch those errors and fix them before they cost you sales and the trust of your customers.

If everything is working, it's time to start sending traffic to your offer. Email your list, announce it on your blog and social media, recruit some affiliates, and call in some favors. Do what you can to send targeted traffic to your sales page. This will be a continuous effort going forward. For now though, sit back and watch the sales starting to trickle in. Pat yourself on the back for a job well done.

Where To Go From Here

I hinted at this in the last chapter. The job isn't quite done, and there's a lot of other things you can do going forward to improve your bottom line. The first is, of course, to continually send more traffic to your sales page, but it doesn't end there. Here are a few more ideas for things you can do going forward to improve your info product business.

Follow Up With Your Customers

Your list of paying customers is one of the most valuable assets your information business has. Make sure you capture your buyer's email address at the point of sale. Shopping carts and shopping cart platforms will do this for you. If you're using a simple PayPal button, it may be time to get a little creative with your auto-responder service and include a signup form for your list on the download page. You can simply invite customers to sign up to receive product updates and related offers.

Then start following up with your customers. Make sure they know how to download and use your product. This will significantly reduce your refund rate and create trust. Then start making other offers and share great content with them. These offers can be other products you create and release, or they can be things you're promoting as an affiliate. This follow-up alone can substantially increase the profitability of your information product business.

Create An Entire Product Funnel

Creating your first product is a good start, but it's just that, a beginning. As soon as your first product is finished, it's time to think about what your customers need next. It helps to map out an entire product funnel that goes from that initial small and low-cost product to high-end information products and coaching offers. Take your customers on a journey with you and help them grow. Here's an example of a simple product funnel for the flower shop business owner we talked about earlier. It starts with simple, lower cost guides and then moves into more involved and thus higher priced products.

- Why Your Flower Shop Needs An Online Presence (this could be a free lead generator)

- Capturing Your Customer's Email Addresses And Keep Bringing Them Back Through Email Marketing

- Tapping Into The Power of Groupon And Other Online Coupon Guides

- A Simple Guide To Social Media For Local Business Owners

- How To Draw In New Business Through Facebook Advertising

- Setting Up A Website And Online Shop For Easy Ordering And Flower Delivery

- Group Coaching – Grow Your Online Presence And Increase Sales For Your Flower Shop

- One On One Coaching – Improving Your Bottom Line With Online Sales

- VIP Coaching Days – Intensive, 3 Day Event, to analyze every part of your online business and come up with a detailed action plan for you to implement.

Do you see how this product funnel moves customers from a free signup to the first low-cost info product, through a series of more involved and higher prices products? You're not going to sell someone on your higher priced products the first time they find you and your information business. Instead, you guide them through this product funnel, show them that you know what you're talking about and can help them. As trust grows, and they start to see results, they'll be ready to spend more and more.

The Magic Of Cross Sales

Of course, products don't always have to get more and more pricey and involved. Another good strategy is to make cross sales. Think of related, similarly priced products you can create or find and offer to your existing customers. Think about what else they need to know or learn. Keep working on more new products and offering them to your client base and your target market in general. As your customer base grows so will the cross sales you make. The email follow up we talked about earlier is a perfect place to make these cross-sale offers.

Implement An Affiliate Program And Work Out Some JV Deals

Now is also a very good time to set up an affiliate program and invite others to promote your product. The most time-consuming part of running a digital product business is marketing your products. As a rule of thumb, you want to spend 20 percent of your time creating the products and 80 percent selling them. Having affiliates do some of the marketing for you helps you make more sales overall and frees you up for more product creation.

JV or joint venture partners are people with a large existing presence with your target audience. Consider creating a special offer for them, or giving them a bigger cut of the profits than regular affiliates to entice them to mail for you.

Consider Creating Memberships Or Coaching Programs For Recurring Income

Last but not least, consider generating recurring revenue by offering a digital product that your customers will pay for month after month. They sign up, and the payment automatically comes out once a month. This could be a membership where they get access to all your info products and training programs, it could be a service where you create their monthly newsletter and email marketing campaign for them or provide them with templates and ideas, or it could be a coaching program. Get creative and see what you can come up with that people would pay you for as a monthly membership.

Above all, keep working on new products, improving your sales and download pages, and continuing to look for new ways to reach your target audience and send more traffic into your product funnel. That first digital product is a great start, but it's hard to make a decent income with one product. Instead, look at it as the start of your very own digital product empire.

CONCLUSION

We've covered a lot of ground in this short little guide on how to create info products. By now you have a good understanding of what digital products are and how you can go about creating them. I'm sure you also have quite a few ideas for products you can create. Maybe you've even started to work on the first one. If not, make that a top priority this week. Make a decision on what your first information product will be and get to work.

Keep referring to this guide as you move along. Spend some time discovering who your target audience is and what they want and need. Base your product ideas on that information, and you'll do well. Your next step will be to choose a format and then come up with a rough draft or outline for what you want to cover. With that done, it's time to buckle down and get the work done. Don't forget to edit and polish your digital product before converting it to a downloadable file.

With your product creation finished, you'll be creating the infrastructure to make a sale possible. Keep it simple and don't forget to test the order process to make sure it works the way you expected it to work. Then make the offer live, tell your target audience about it and get those first few sales. If you keep it simple and create a small product, you can easily get all this accomplished over the course of a week or two. I challenge you to get it done and learn the process of info product creation. From there, you'll be ready to move into some of the more advanced strategies we discussed in the last chapter and continue to grow your digital product business. Good luck and remember anything new is hard at first.

Information product creation will become easier with each new product you finish and put out there.

As a final thought, take a look at these top ten tips for creating digital products:

1. Figure out who your target audience is. Once you know that, you'll have a much better idea of what product to create

2. Decide on what format your product will be in - Audio, Video, Written etc.

3. Define or find a problem your target audience has and then provide them with a product that solves the problem

4. Create the content yourself or pay someone to create it for you if you don't have the necessary skills to do it yourself

5. Create a compelling sales page that highlights the benefits of your product

6. Make it easy for people to download the product - include instructions if necessary

7. Select a way to take payments for your digital products - PayPal is the easiest to get started with

8. Test everything to make sure it all works as it should before making the offer live

9. Follow up with customers 10.Keep creating new products

Printed by Libri Plureos GmbH in Hamburg, Germany